Dates of a Decade

THE 1990s

Anne Rooney

with additional text by Jacqueline Laks Gorman

ARCTURUS

This edition first published by Arcturus Publishing
Distributed by Black Rabbit Books
123 South Broad Street
Mankato
Minnesota MN 56001

Copyright © 2009 Arcturus Publishing Limited

Printed in the United States

All rights reserved

Series concept: Alex Woolf
Editor and picture researcher: Alex Woolf
U.S. editor: Jacqueline Laks Gorman
Designer: Phipps Design

Library of Congress Cataloging-in-Publication Data

Rooney, Anne.
  The 1990s / Anne Rooney.
      p. cm. -- (Dates of a decade)
  Includes index.
  ISBN 978-1-84837-285-6 (hardcover)
  1. History, Modern--1989---Juvenile literature. I. Title.

D856.R665 2010
909.82'9--dc22
                                          2009000009

Picture credits:
Corbis: 4 (NASA/Roger Ressmeyer), 5 (Reuters), 6 (Durand-Hudson-Langevin-Orban/Sygma), 7 (Peter Turnley), 9 (Les Stone/Sygma), 11 (Pallava Bagla), 12 (Peter Turnley), 13 (Steve Raymer), 14 (Reuters), 16 (Louise Gubb), 17 (Jeremiah Kamau/Reuters), cover *center* and 19 (Peter Turnley), 22 (Tokyo Shimbun/Sygma), 24 (Patrick Robert/Sygma), 25 (Patrick Robert/Sygma), 26 (David Turnley), 28 (Reuters), cover *right* and 31 (Najlah Feanny-Hicks), 33 (Langevin Jacques), 36 (Najlah Feanny-Hicks), 39 (Remi Benali), 41 (Reuters), 42 (Larry Downing/Sygma), 43 (James Leynse), 44 (Martin H. Simon).
Getty Images: cover *left*, 8 (AFP), 15 (AFP), 20 (AFP), 21 (AFP), 23 (AFP), 27 (AFP), 29, 32 (AFP), 35 (AFP), 37, 45.
PA Photos: 40 (David Longstreath/AP).

Contents

GLOBAL EVENTS

UNITED STATES EVENTS

The Hubble Space Telescope Is Launched

Seventy years after a telescope in space was first suggested, the shuttle Discovery blasted into space carrying the Hubble Space Telescope. It had been built as a joint project by NASA and the European Space Agency (ESA). The size of a school bus, the telescope was positioned in orbit above the Earth. From there, it would collect the clearest pictures ever seen of distant stars and galaxies. Scientists from all over the world booked time with Hubble to assist them in their projects. It quickly became a valuable tool for science everywhere.

The Hubble Space Telescope is retrieved by the space shuttle Endeavor so that astronauts can carry out repairs.

Light from the stars is processed by instruments on board Hubble. Information and images are sent by radio link to Earth. The same link is used to control the telescope. Designed to stay in space for 15 years, Hubble is serviced, repaired, and improved by astronauts and robots. This was put to the test early on: a tiny manufacturing fault in one of Hubble's mirrors had to be corrected by astronauts in 1993 before Hubble could send back crystal-clear images.

Staring into space

The world was soon stunned by the astonishing photographs from Hubble. For the first time, astronomers could see detailed images of galaxies unimaginable distances from Earth. The images from Hubble are ten times clearer than anything that can be seen from the ground, since Earth's atmosphere absorbs, reflects, and distorts light from space. Images of distant objects are also images from distant times. The light from other galaxies has taken millions or billions of years to reach Earth. Some of the distant objects Hubble has photographed may no longer even exist. Hubble revealed how stars form, age, and eventually die, expanding massively into red giants before finally running out of energy and cooling. Astronomers have even seen circles of dust collecting around stars. The dust will eventually clump together to form planets. With Hubble, we can watch the history of our own solar system played out in other planetary systems far away.

Visiting the stars without leaving Earth

Since the moon missions in the 1960s, humans have not ventured outside Earth's orbit, but unmanned probes have gone much further afield. In 1990, the probe Magellan began sending back images of Venus from its mission to map the planet. In 1997, the Mars rover Sojourner began its exploration of Mars, taking photographs and collecting and analyzing samples of rock and dust.

This photo is one of many taken by the Hubble Space Telescope, offering astronomers fascinating new insights into the cosmos. This shows the Omega or Swan Nebula, an area where new stars are formed, some 5,500 light years from Earth in the constellation Sagittarius.

● eye witness

Every image taken will be an image not of the universe as it is now, but as it was at, say, half its present age – before the solar system was formed. You're really going far back in time to understand the evolutionary processes by which the universe got to its present state. So many better questions are being asked now than 25 years ago ... and with machines such as the space telescope we can actually begin to hope to get answers.

Professor Malcolm Longair, the Astronomer Royal for Scotland, 1990

- **SEE ALSO**
  Pages 20–21: May 6, 1994
  The Channel Tunnel Opens

  Pages 30–31: July 5, 1996
  Dolly the Sheep Is Born

- **FURTHER INFORMATION**
  📖 Books:
  Hubble: 15 Years of Discovery by Christensen Lars Lindberg, Robert A Fosbury, and Martin Kornmesser (Springer-Verlag, 2006)
  🖰 Websites:
  hubblesite.org/
  Hubble's official website

Iraq Invades Kuwait

The people of the small Gulf state of Kuwait slept peacefully in the early hours of August 2, 1990, unaware that their country was being invaded. Over 100,000 troops and 700 tanks from neighboring Iraq crossed the border and quickly took control. The emir, the leader of Kuwait, escaped immediately into Saudi Arabia, a country friendly toward Western nations such as the United States and Britain. The Iraqi leader, Saddam Hussein, threatened to turn the country's capital, Kuwait City, into a graveyard if other nations tried to stop his army.

Events quickly escalated. Foreign powers decided it was important to liberate Kuwait and protect neighboring Saudi Arabia. U.S. troops began to arrive within days of the invasion to protect the border of Saudi Arabia in an operation called Desert Shield. The Security Council of the United Nations imposed economic sanctions on Iraq and demanded that the country withdraw its troops from Kuwait. Led by the United States and Britain, a coalition of forces from 34 countries closed in on Iraq.

U.S. Marines prepare to blow up a portrait of Iraqi leader Saddam Hussein in Al Jahrah, north-western Kuwait.

Oil and land

Kuwait had originally been part of Basra, an area of Iraq, but became a separate territory in 1922. Iraq finally accepted Kuwait's independence in 1963, but the two nations continued to dispute their border. For Iraq, there was more at stake than land. Both Iraq and Kuwait had become wealthy from selling oil to the rest of the world. Iraq claimed that Kuwait was selling too much oil, pushing down the price, and even taking some of it from Iraqi oil fields.

Low oil prices hit Iraq hard. Saddam Hussein believed the United States would not interfere in an invasion of Kuwait. He was wrong. The United States led the assault on the occupying Iraqi forces.

All-out war

The deadline for withdrawal ended on January 15, 1991, yet Iraqi forces continued to occupy Kuwait. Two days later, coalition forces launched the longest air strike in military history. Called Desert Storm, the assault targeted Iraqi troops and installations in Kuwait and military and civilian targets inside Iraq. Iraq launched missiles against Israel and Saudi Arabia, both states with strong ties to the West.

The war lasted six weeks. Defeat came for Iraq at the end of February 1991. As Iraqi troops retreated from Kuwait City on the night of February 26-27, U.S. fighter planes bombed them continuously. The road from the city became known as the Highway of Death. Although Iraq called for a ceasefire, no formal peace agreement was ever reached, leaving the way open for future conflict.

Highway of Death: as Iraqi military personnel and their families fled Kuwait, they came under air assault from coalition forces. The attack left hundreds of destroyed vehicles littering the highway from Kuwait to Iraq.

⊙ **eye** witness

My wife and children were shocked at the destruction that was so close to our house, now they could understand all the shelling, booming and rattling of windows for two days and most importantly why they had to remain away from windows. As we rode in, almost every official Kuwait government building along the route had been shelled, torched, or destroyed. Wrecked and smoldering vehicles littered the highway some with the charred remains present. The once well manicured and green medians were now brown, dried up and trashed.

LTC Fred L. Hart, Jr., a U.S. military adviser to the Kuwaiti Land Forces, who witnessed the Iraqi invasion

- **SEE ALSO**
  Pages 14–15: September 13, 1993
  Peace in the Middle East?

- **FURTHER INFORMATION**
  📖 Books:
  Persian Gulf War by Kathlyn and Martin Gay (Twenty-First Century Books, 1996)
  The Gulf War by Suzanne J. Murdico (Rosen Publishing Group, 2004)
  🖱 Websites:
  www.pbs.org/wgbh/pages/frontline/gulf/
  Chronology of the invasion and subsequent war

Eruption of Mount Pinatubo

On June 15, 1991 a massive eruption blew away the summit of the volcano Pinatubo, devastating the island of Luzon in the Philippines. A column of scorching ash, gases, and lava (molten rock) blasted 21 miles (34 kilometers) into the air. The eruption hurled ash and lava over an area of 48,000 square miles (125,000 square kilometers). Searing winds rushed from the volcano, destroying everything in their path. Ash lay 2 inches (5 centimeters) deep around the volcano and even fell as far away as Cambodia and Vietnam. It was the second largest eruption of the century and killed 300 people.

At the same time, a tropical storm struck the island. The wind and rain combined with the falling ash to make deadly mud flows called lahars, which can travel at up to 40 miles (65 kilometers) per hour. Most of those who died were crushed by roofs collapsing under the weight of wet ash.

A sleeping giant wakes

Pinatubo had lain dormant for 500 years, and the 30,000 people living on its forested slopes had no idea their homes were on a volcano until 1990. After an earthquake on July 16, struck the center of the island, a series of small earthquakes and eruptions signalled that the volcano was waking up. Activity increased in the spring and early summer

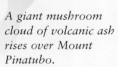

A giant mushroom cloud of volcanic ash rises over Mount Pinatubo.

Five months after the eruption of Mount Pinatubo, Santa Barbara Elementary School on Luzon still lies buried up to its roof in volcanic ash. The eruption caused widespread damage to buildings and infrastructure and left 250,000 people homeless.

of 1991 and became much more violent in early June, with eruptions of lava and ash. By June 14, 60,000 people had left the area around the volcano and 18,000 had left a nearby air base.

Lasting effects

The final eruption threw so much ash, dust, and gas into the atmosphere that global temperatures dropped by about 0.9°F (0.5°C) and took two years to recover. Five years later, whole valleys on Luzon were still filled with deep piles of ash, some of it as hot as 932°F (500°C). It could stay scorching hot for decades. Lahars are still occurring and have destroyed 100,000 homes. The sloppy volcanic mud forms into huge lakes. When the sediment settles, the water eventually breaks out without warning and the flood causes another lahar.

A decade of disasters

Mount Unzen, in Japan, erupted a week before Pinatubo, killing 35 people. A series of devastating earthquakes shook the world in the 1990s, too. Iran suffered its worst-ever natural disaster on June 17, 1990, when an earthquake killed 50,000 people and injured 100,000. Earthquakes in India on September 30, 1993 killed up to 22,000 people, and on January 17, 1995, the largest earthquake to strike Japan in more than 70 years killed 6,432 in Kobe.

What the papers said

The greatest threats to human lives may come from overlooked, long dormant volcanoes. To monitor a volcano requires identifying it beforehand; as recently as 1981, Pinatubo was not even included in the worldwide registry of volcanoes maintained by the Smithsonian Institution. "When a nice little hill covered with lush vegetation finally wakes up," observes Smithsonian volcanologist Tom Simkin, "it's going to cause a lot of damage."

Time, June 24, 1991

- **SEE ALSO**
Pages 24–25: May 6, 1995
Ebola Fever Strikes in Africa

- **FURTHER INFORMATION**
  📖 Books:
  Volcano by Anne Rooney
  (Dorling Kindersley, 2006)
  🖰 Websites:
  park.org/Philippines/pinatubo/index.html
  An account of the eruption

The World Wide Web Goes Live

The first click on hyperlinked text to go from one page to another over the Internet happened in Switzerland on August 6, 1991. The World Wide Web began at that moment. Over a few short years, it would grow into a global network of shared information on every imaginable topic.

The invention was the work of Tim Berners-Lee, a British researcher at the CERN laboratory in Geneva, Switzerland. He had set out to help physics researchers at CERN to share their work seamlessly by linking their papers together on a network of computers. But he soon realized the concept could be extended to any information, anywhere in the world, by using the Internet to move the information around. (The Internet itself had existed since 1969, when it began as ARPANET, a network created for the U.S. Defense Department.)

In early 1991, physics departments in a number of European universities shared the first web pages on a private network. In August 1991, Berners-Lee released his invention to the world using the Internet. The first web page had the address info.cern.ch/hypertext/WWW/TheProject.html. But just a single web server was no use. The Web depended on other people putting up their own websites and linking them together.

eye witness

In August I released three things – the *WorldWideWeb* for NeXT, the line-mode browser, and the basic server for any machine – outside CERN by making them all available on the Internet. I posted a notice on several Internet newsgroups, chief among them alt.hypertext.... Putting the Web out on alt.hypertext was a watershed event. It exposed the Web to a very critical academic community. I began to get e-mail from people.... "Hey, I've just set up a server, and it's dead cool. Here's the address."

Tim Berners-Lee, *Weaving the Web* (Orion Business Books, 1999)

Up and running – fast

Berners-Lee developed tools other people could use to make and view web pages. A physics laboratory in Stanford, California, set up the first web server outside Europe. By November 1992, there were 26 servers in the world. A year later, there were more than 200. Berners-Lee invited other people to produce software for the Web. The Mosaic browser, developed in 1993, proved popular. It would eventually turn into Internet Explorer. With good browsers for popular PC and

*Robert Cailliau (left) with
the original NeXT computer terminal on
which the World Wide Web was created. Calliau
worked with Berners-Lee on the project.*

Macintosh computers, the Web took off rapidly. By the end of 1993 there
were at least 500 web servers. By the end of 1994, there were 10,000, and
10 million users.

Changing face of the Web

The very first web pages were nothing like modern web pages.
Pages could not yet mix text and pictures. There were no
sound, video, animations, or fancy text designs. But
as more people started to use the Web, it rapidly
evolved and more features appeared. Private
individuals started using the Web and even
buying computers just so they could use it. Soon,
people were using the Web for business, education,
entertainment, personal communication and
shopping. Within a single decade, the existence
of the World Wide Web transformed business
and social life around the world.

- **SEE ALSO**
  Pages 4–5: April 24, 1990
  The Hubble Space Telescope Is Launched
  Pages 20–21: May 6, 1994
  The Channel Tunnel Opens
  Pages 30–31: July 5, 1996
  Dolly the Sheep Is Born

- **FURTHER INFORMATION**
  📖 Books:
  Tim Berners-Lee: Inventor of the World Wide Web
  by Niall Fergusson (Facts on File, 2001)
  🖱 Websites:
  news.bbc.co.uk/1/hi/technology/5242252.stm
  How the Web went worldwide

The End of the Soviet Union

The Soviet Union finally came to a peaceful end on December 8, 1991. The communist state had been in severe decline for most of the 1980s. Its state-run economy was very inefficient. Also, the Soviet Union could no longer compete with the United States, its main military rival. Mikhail Gorbachev (ruled 1985–1991) tried to reform the economy, but his attempt came too late and was poorly managed. He only succeeded in weakening the country even more.

By the late 1980s, several of the republics that made up the Soviet Union began to push for independence. In August 1991, hard-line communists tried to overthrow Gorbachev and reverse the changes he had made. The coup failed, but the republics realized that they would be better off as independent states.

On December 8, 1991, the leaders of three republics, Russia, Belarus, and the Ukraine, signed the Belavezha Accords, dissolving the Soviet Union. The remaining republics completed the process by signing the Alma-Ata Protocol on December 21, 1991. The 15 newly independent states agreed to form a loose confederation called the Commonwealth of Independent States (CIS).

During the attempted coup of August 1991, Boris Yeltsin stands defiantly in front of the Russian parliament building, refusing to surrender the government to the coup leaders.

Ending 80 years of communism

The Soviet Union was formed in 1922, five years after the overthrow of the tsar in the Russian Revolution. It was a one-party communist state, with power concentrated in the hands of the ruling Communist Party. People were not allowed to own private property and the state controlled the economy and all trade.

After World War II, tension mounted between the Soviet Union and the United States. The Soviet Union took control of Eastern Europe, exercising its authority through communist puppet regimes. The world divided into two hostile camps, one allied to the Soviet Union and the other with the United States – a period known as the Cold War. In 1989, Gorbachev ended Soviet control of Eastern Europe. The communist states there swiftly collapsed, ending the Cold War.

After communism

After 1991, Russia, the dominant republic of the former Soviet Union, moved quickly toward a free market economy. The change was not well managed. Prices rose out of control, and basic goods such as food and clothing were in short supply. While a few people grew very wealthy, most Russians had a low standard of living. Corruption and crime were everywhere, with organized gangs running many businesses.

In 1994, the province of Chechnya declared independence from Russia, leading to a war (1994–1996) in which 50,000 people died. The newly independent Chechen state was lawless and chaotic, and war broke out again in 1999–2000.

Hard times in post-communist Russia: a homeless woman and child huddle under a ledge on Nevsky Prospekt in the city of St. Petersburg.

- **SEE ALSO**
  Pages 26–27: July 12, 1995
  Massacre at Srebrenica

- **FURTHER INFORMATION**
  Books:
  The Rise and Fall of the Soviet Union edited by Laurie S Stoff (Greenhaven Press, 2005)
  Websites:
  news.bbc.co.uk/onthisday/hi/dates/stories/december/25/newsid_2542000/2542749.stm
  Gorbachev's resignation and the break-up of the Soviet Union

What the papers said

The Soviet Union died after a long illness which took a decisive turn for the worse some time during 1989. The moment of death went unnoticed because of the massacre of its Eastern European relatives. We are left with a zombie. It makes little sense to rejoice in dismembering it, particularly into parts that still have the power of regeneration.

Sunday Times, December 8, 1991

Peace in the Middle East?

Peace in the Middle East finally looked possible with the signing of the Oslo Accords on the lawn of the White House in Washington, D.C. Since Israel was established in 1948, the Jewish state had been in conflict with the Arab world. The Accords were reached in Oslo, Norway, on August 20, 1993 and signed in the United States a month later by Yasser Arafat, leader of the Palestine Liberation Organization (PLO), and Yitzhak Rabin, prime minister of Israel.

Ancient claims

Traditionally, the Jewish people have felt a sacred attachment to the land now occupied by Israel. It had been a Jewish kingdom in Biblical times, and Jews believe the land was promised to them by God. From the late 19th century, Jews escaping persecution in Russia and Europe began settling the land. By then it was known as Palestine and was part of the Turkish Ottoman Empire. As the numbers of Jewish settlers grew, they came into increasing conflict with the Arab Muslims (Palestinians) living there.

Establishment of Israel

At the end of World War I, the Ottoman Empire collapsed and Britain took charge of Palestine, with the purpose of establishing a Jewish homeland there. In the 1930s, large numbers of Jews

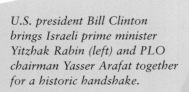

U.S. president Bill Clinton brings Israeli prime minister Yitzhak Rabin (left) and PLO chairman Yasser Arafat together for a historic handshake.

● eye witness

The horizons to peace are open. There is a stirring in the entire Arab arena in their readiness to make peace. Not that there aren't obstacles, not that there aren't difficulties. But I'm convinced that the horizons to peace are open.

Yitzhak Rabin, in a speech to the Israeli parliament, 1993

arrived, many fleeing the Holocaust in Europe. The British rulers struggled to control the increasing violence between Jewish settlers and Palestinians. Britain decided to give up its mandate in 1947. The United Nations planned to divide Palestine into two states, one Jewish, one Arab, with Jerusalem an international city. The Jewish community accepted the plan; the Palesinians did not. When Israel was founded in May 1948, the neighboring Arab states immediately declared war. By 1949, Israel had triumphed.

Palestinian-Israeli conflict

In 1967, Israel won another war and occupied additional territories, including the Gaza Strip and the West Bank (known thereafter as the occupied territories). After 1967, the PLO rose to the forefront of the Palestinian struggle. The PLO frequently used terrorism as a means of pursuing its aims. The conflict continued, with few opportunities for peace, until the 1990s.

Continuing conflict: a Jewish settler fires warning shots after Palestinians set fire to a construction site near the settlement of Beit El on the West Bank in August 1995.

Toward peace

The Oslo Accords represented a breakthrough. For the first time, Palestinians acknowledged the right of Israel to exist. The parties also agreed to the creation of a Palestine National Authority, with civil (though not military) authority over parts of the occupied territories. Israel and the PLO agreed to resolve their remaining differences through negotiation, not armed conflict. These included the status of Jerusalem, Jewish settlements in the occupied territories, and the right of Palestinian refugees to return to Israel.

Despite a promising start, the Oslo Accords did not provide an easy path to peace. During the later 1990s, terrorist attacks by Palestinian groups such as Hamas eroded support for the peace process in Israel. Jewish settlements continued to be built in the occupied territories, inflaming Arab opinion. A renewed attempt to reach peace in 2000 failed.

- **SEE ALSO**
  Pages 6–7: August 2, 1990
  Iraq Invades Kuwait

- **FURTHER INFORMATION**
  📖 Books:
  Causes and Consequences: The Arab-Israeli Conflict by Stewart Ross (Evans, 2004)
  🖥 Websites:
  news.bbc.co.uk/cbbcnews/hi/newsid_
  1600000/newsid_1602700/1602748.stm
  A guide to the Israeli-Palestinian conflict

Genocide in Rwanda

When unknown killers shot down a plane carrying two African presidents, it sparked violence that quickly turned into genocide. The world stood by while 800,000 people were butchered. The two presidents were Juvénal Habyarimana of Rwanda, a small state in Central Africa, and Cyprien Ntaryamira of neighboring Burundi. They were on their way home from peace talks between representatives of the rival Tutsi and Hutu tribes. Their journey ended anything but peacefully. Both men were members of the Hutu tribe. The Hutus assumed a Tutsi had shot down their plane, and they launched a pitiless assault on the Tutsis in Rwanda.

Two tribes

Rwanda and Burundi had once been a single country, ruled by Belgium and home to both Hutus and Tutsis. The Belgians favored the Tutsis over the Hutus, causing tension between the groups. When the Hutus rioted and killed 20,000 Tutsis in 1959, Belgium withdrew and two new countries were formed. Most Hutus settled in Rwanda, and most Tutsis in Burundi.

A group of Tutsis in Uganda wanted to overthrow Habyarimana and return to Rwanda. They formed the Rwandan Patriotic Front (RPF). In Rwanda, Habyarimana persecuted the Tutsis, accusing them of being RPF sympathizers. He made peace with the RPF in August 1993, but when he was assassinated, the Hutus blamed the Tutsis and turned on them.

A child looks at the remains of some 25,000 Tutsis, and some Hutus, who were massacred in and around the Nyamata Catholic church and in the surrounding Kanzenze community in Rwanda.

Massacre

Within hours, the presidential guard murdered opposition political leaders and sent troops to slaughter Tutsis throughout the country. An unofficial Hutu group, the Interahamwe, swept through the country murdering, raping, and mutilating Tutsis. Police and soldiers led the slaughter, but ordinary citizens were

Some of the 250,000 Rwandan refugees who crossed the border into Tanzania, following the massacre.

quickly recruited or forced to join in. At its height, the Interahamwe had 30,000 members. Over a period of 100 days, they killed 800,000 Tutsis.

The international community did nothing to prevent the massacre. UN forces withdrew after ten UN soldiers died. In July, the RPF captured the capital, Kigali, and imposed a ceasefire. Terrified that they would now suffer in turn, 2 million Hutus fled the country. They poured into neighboring Zaire (now the Democratic Republic of Congo), causing a humanitarian crisis – there was nowhere for them to go but refugee camps with insufficient food and no medical aid. In July, a new government, with a Hutu president and many RPF ministers, promised a safe return for all refugees.

Investigations continued for years after the massacre. Ten years later, 100,000 people were still in prison and 500 had been executed for their parts in the massacre. However, many of the massacre's ringleaders escaped justice.

eye witness

People were sliced to pieces with machetes and axes, skulls crushed with rocks and children tied in sacks and tossed into rivers…. In the banana fields there are more dead bodies than bananas. This can only be compared to what the Nazis did.

Anonymous witness to the massacre

- **SEE ALSO**
  Pages 18–19: April 27, 1994
  Black Rule in South Africa
  Pages 26–27: July 12, 1995
  Massacre at Srebrenica

- **FURTHER INFORMATION**
  Books:
  Rwanda: Country Torn Apart by Kari Bodnarchuk (Lerner Publishing Group, 2001)
  The Rwanda Genocide by Christina Fisanick (Greenhaven Press, 2004)
  Websites:
  news.bbc.co.uk/1/hi/in_depth/africa/2004/rwanda/default.stm
  A review of the genocide 10 years later

Black Rule in South Africa

Joyful scenes greeted the election of Nelson Mandela as the first black president of South Africa on April 27, 1994. After 27 years in jail, Mandela was finally freed in 1990. With the first free elections in South Africa's history, Mandela now saw his dream of freedom for black people come true. His election as president ended more than a century of unfair treatment of the black majority by the white minority in South Africa. The African National Congress party (ANC), which Mandela led, won 252 of the 400 seats in the South African parliament.

Apartheid

The position of black people in South Africa had turned around completely in less than a decade. Since the birth of South Africa in 1910, the white population, of European descent, had oppressed the black majority. This racial discrimination became formalized in 1948 when the National Party introduced a system known as apartheid, which forced black and white people to live and work apart. From the 1960s, black people were made to move into "homelands" and townships, poor shanty towns on the outskirts of the more prosperous cities. Black people had few rights and were not considered citizens of South Africa.

The ANC campaigned peacefully at first, and then more violently, against apartheid. The government outlawed the ANC, and Mandela was imprisoned for life in 1962. In jail, he became the figurehead of the movement to end apartheid, supported around the world.

By the end of the 1980s, the combined pressures of internal rebellion and international isolation finally forced the South African government to make concessions. In 1989, the ban on the ANC was lifted, and in 1990, Mandela was freed. He worked with the South African President F. W. de Klerk to dismantle the apartheid system and establish South Africa as a multiracial democracy. They achieved that goal with the elections of 1994. Mandela and De Klerk were jointly awarded the Nobel Prize for Peace in 1993.

eye witness

Let there be justice for all.
Let there be peace for all.
Let there be work, bread, water and salt for all.
Let each know that for each the body, the mind and the soul have been freed to fulfil themselves.
Never, never and never again shall it be that this beautiful land will again experience the oppression of one by another and suffer the indignity of being the skunk of the world.

Nelson Mandela, May 10, 1994

A difficult path

Winning the election was a huge step forward for South Africa, but the country still had to deal with the legacy of its violent and divided past. Under the leadership of Bishop Desmond Tutu, the Truth and Reconciliation Commission set about investigating and acknowledging the terrible things that had happened in the recent past. They intended not to blame or punish people, but to bring events out into the open and enable the country to move on from a position of honesty.

South Africa also faced other difficulties. The years of apartheid had left the country isolated and poor. The new government had to struggle with the poverty suffered by most of the black population, the terrible housing shortage, and the squalor of the townships. The country was also ravaged by HIV/AIDS. Currently, one in five people in South Africa is infected.

Former political prisoner Nelson Mandela campaigns for the presidency of South Africa.

- **SEE ALSO**
  Pages 16–17: April 6, 1994
  Genocide in Rwanda
  Pages 32–33: July 1, 1997
  Hong Kong Returns to China

- **FURTHER INFORMATION**
  Books:
  Apartheid in South Africa by David Downing (Heinemann, 2005)
  Websites:
  www.pbs.org/wgbh/pages/frontline/shows/mandela/
  Mandela's life and triumph.

The Channel Tunnel Opens

On May 6, 1994, it became possible to travel from England to France without crossing water for the first time since the end of the last ice age, nearly 10,000 years ago. That day saw the opening of the Channel Tunnel, a rail tunnel beneath the English Channel, the sea between England and France. It allows trains to travel between London and Paris in just three hours. Other trains, called Le Shuttle, carry road vehicles under the Channel between Kent and northern France in only 35 minutes.

The dream of a tunnel beneath the Channel began in 1802 when Albert Mathieu-Favier suggested a tunnel for horse-drawn carriages, lit by oil lamps. In 1875, both the British and French governments gave the go-ahead to build a tunnel, but the money was not available. Building stopped and started several times between 1922 and 1975, until the idea was relaunched in 1984. A formal treaty was signed on February 12, 1986, and work began in 1988.

May 6, 1994: the Eurostar Channel Tunnel train pulls out of the international terminal at Waterloo Station on its first journey.

What the media said

The Queen embarked on today's historic journey from the new Channel Tunnel terminal in London's Waterloo Station accompanied by much of her government and other leading British politicians. Her Majesty was to travel in the new Eurostar passenger train along the first land link between Britain and the Continent since the Ice Age…. With a full commercial service still perhaps nine months away, serious doubts hang over its long-term financial viability.

Mike Smart, BBC News, May 6, 1994

French and English workers shake hands after a giant drilling machine broke through the last section of ground separating the English and French halves of the Channel Tunnel.

A major feat of engineering

The Channel Tunnel – or Chunnel – is the second longest tunnel in the world, after the Seikan Tunnel in Japan, and is the longest undersea tunnel. The Chunnel is actually three tunnels running side by side. One carries trains from France to England, another carries trains from England to France, and a service tunnel runs between them. It took 30,000 construction workers seven years to complete the tunnel. Most of it is 131 feet (40 meters) under the sea bed. It was started from both ends, using laser surveying tools to make sure the two tunnels were lined up. When they met, the center lines of the two tunnels were out of alignment by only 15 inches (358 millimeters) horizontally and 2.3 inches (58 millimeters) vertically.

Unwelcome guests

When the Chunnel first opened, some people in Britain worried that the disease rabies would spread from Europe to Britain, carried through the service tunnel by animals. Britain is rabies-free, so electrified grids, tracking, and security measures were used to stop wildlife entering the tunnel from France. As rabies control in Europe has improved, the barriers have been removed.

In 1999, the Sangatte refugee camp opened near Calais. Many refugees escaped from the camp and tried to get into Britain illegally by hiding on freight trains heading for Britain through the Channel Tunnel. Several suffered injuries or died attempting to jump onto trains. The camp was closed in 2002.

- **SEE ALSO**
Pages 10–11: August 6, 1991
The World Wide Web Goes Live
Pages 30–31: July 5, 1996
Dolly the Sheep is Born

- **FURTHER INFORMATION**
  📖 Books:
  The Channel Tunnel by S. Donovan (Lerner Publishing Group, 2003)
  🖱 Websites:
  www.theotherside.co.uk/tm-heritage/background/tunnel.htm
  A history of the Channel Tunnel from the first plans

Nerve Gas Attack on the Tokyo Subway

People fled from the Tokyo subway system and collapsed as a deadly nerve gas spread through five stations during the early morning rush hour. The sarin gas was released by members of the religious group Aum Shinrikyo ("Supreme Truth") in the most serious assault in Japan since World War II. Twelve people died and 50 were seriously injured. Five thousand have suffered lasting health problems.

Each member of the group had a bag of sarin wrapped in newspaper. At a prearranged time, they each dropped a bag on the floor and punctured it with a sharpened umbrella. The sarin liquid evaporated and spread as a gas, breathed in by people nearby. Altogether, the group used a quart of sarin. A single drop the size of a pinhead is enough to kill an adult.

Panic – and good fortune

At first, no one knew why the people pouring out of the stations were so ill. The cause was discovered by chance. A doctor who had helped victims of a previous sarin attack on a town outside Tokyo saw the news coverage on television and recognized the symptoms. He contacted the hospital in Tokyo where most of the victims had been taken and told doctors that sarin poisoning was the cause.

A commuter crouches on a subway platform beside a victim of the sarin gas attack. The gas was released on three different lines of the Tokyo subway during the morning rush hour.

Sarin is a nerve toxin. It interrupts messages going to and from the brain. Victims have disturbed vision and breathing difficulties. They eventually die of suffocation.

As panic spread, many people who were unaffected went to hospitals demanding to be checked. These "worried well" clogged the hospitals, making it more difficult for medical workers to identify and treat those who were genuinely ill. The incident highlighted problems in emergency planning in Tokyo.

Aum Shinrikyo

Aum Shinrikyo is a religious sect with links to the criminal underworld, including the Japanese mafia, Yakuza. Leaders of Aum taught that the end of the world was approaching and only members of Aum Shinrikyo would survive. The group turned to violence after failing to win seats in the 1989 elections in Japan.

Police raided Aum Shinrikyo premises after the attack and found a massive chemical weapons factory. The group had even sent a team to Zaire in 1994 to collect samples of Ebola, which they hoped to use as a weapon. An earlier attempt to release poison in Tokyo had failed. Twelve members of Aum were sentenced to death for their parts in the Tokyo attacks.

Shoko Asahara, leader of Aum Shinrikyo and mastermind of the 1995 sarin gas attack.

What the papers said

Six people died and more than 1,300 panic-stricken rush-hour commuters were poisoned today as clouds of lethal nerve gas swept through the crowded Tokyo underground network…. As emergency services and hospitals tried to cope with the enormous stream of choking victims, 16 of whom are critical, the shocked Japanese government denounced the atrocity as "indiscriminate murder"…. With a massive manhunt under way, police revealed that the poison used was Sarin, a nerve gas developed by the Nazis and 20 times more lethal than potassium cyanide.

Evening Standard (London), March 20, 1995

- **SEE ALSO**
  Pages 24–25: May 6, 1995
  Ebola Fever Strikes in Africa
  Pages 36–37: April 20, 1999
  Massacre at Columbine High School
  Pages 40–41: April 19, 1995
  The Oklahoma City Bombing

- **FURTHER INFORMATION**
  Books:
  Chemical and Biological Weapons: Anthrax and Sarin by Gregory Payan (Children's Press, 2000)
  Websites:
  www.discoverychannel.co.uk/reality/ zero_hour/tokyo/index.shtml
  A timeline of the attack on the subway system

06
MAY
1995

Ebola Fever Strikes in Africa

Panic took hold as information filtered out of Africa: people were dying from a terrible disease in Zaire (now the Democratic Republic of Congo). Victims developed fever and vomiting, then began bleeding from the eyes, mouth, nose, and ears. Their internal organs apparently turned to mush and leaked out of their bodies. With no cure or preventive vaccine, people worried that Ebola fever might sweep the world in an unstoppable pandemic. Although Ebola fever did spread rapidly through small communities in Zaire, health authorities managed to bring the outbreak under control within months.

The World Health Organization (WHO) learned of the outbreak on May 6, 1995. By mid-June, more than 200 people had died from the disease. WHO workers went to Zaire to take over the work of caring for victims and burying the dead. Everyone attending the sick or dealing with dead

In Zaire, everyone had to wear full protective clothing when nursing or burying victims of Ebola fever.

bodies wore full protective clothing, goggles, and masks. Many victims of the outbreak were healthcare workers who had treated infected people and had not taken adequate precautions.

Villages were sealed off to prevent people from moving away and possibly carrying the disease with them. These precautions helped to contain the disease, and it did not spread further afield. By the end of the outbreak, 250 people had died – eight out of ten of those who caught the disease.

Ebola fever

Ebola fever first appeared in 1976 in an epidemic that killed 431 people. The first signs are fatigue, weakness, headache, backache, vomiting, and diarrhoea. These symptoms are followed by a rash, then by bleeding from the intestines, leaking from the mouth and rectum. Victims often also bleed from the ears, nose, and eyes. Ebola fever can spread between people, carried in body fluids. It can also be caught from infected animals and used medical equipment. In January 2008, scientists created a "safe" version of the Ebola virus. They hope it can be used to help develop a cure or vaccine.

Professor Jean-Jacques Muyembe-Tamfum was the Zairean doctor in charge of the WHO operation during the 1995 Ebola fever epidemic.

What the papers said

Two Italian nuns working in Zaire have died from a jungle disease that turns body organs into liquid…. The Ebola virus has wiped out entire villages in the former Belgian colony and in Sudan and is among the most dangerous known. Some strains can be transmitted in the air, by bite, or by contact with body fluids. They affect virtually every organ in the body, turning tissues into a highly infectious mush.

The Times, May 10, 1995

- **SEE ALSO**
  Pages 16–17: April 6, 1994
  Genocide in Rwanda
  Pages 22–23: March 20, 1995
  Nerve Gas Attack on the Tokyo Subway

- **FURTHER INFORMATION**
  📖 Books:
  Ebola by Tara C. Smith
  (Chelsea House Publishers, 2006)
  The Ebola Virus by Kris Hirschmann
  (Lucent, 2006)
  🖰 Websites:
  www.bbc.co.uk/radio4/science/ebola.shtml
  Listen to a BBC radio program about Ebola.

Massacre at Srebrenica

The world was horrified to learn of the slaughter and torture of 8,000 men and boys by Serbian forces at Srebrenica, Bosnia – the worst atrocity on European soil since World War II. On July 12, 1995, Serbian troops began a massacre of 8,000 Bosnian Muslim men and boys. In the refugee camp of Potocari, Serb soldiers separated the men and boys from their families and systematically shot them. In the town, people were randomly shot and tortured, and women were raped. Bodies were pushed into mass graves by bulldozers, and some injured people were buried alive. United Nations (UN) soldiers were present but were not authorized to use force and were unable to stop the killing. They had to stand by and allow the massacre to take place.

Balkan conflict

There is a long history of ethnic tensions in the Balkans, the region of southeastern Europe that includes Bosnia. For a long time, Serbia had wanted to be a major force in the region. Serb minorities lived in several surrounding territories, including Bosnia, Croatia, Montenegro, and Kosovo. Serb nationalists wished to unite these regions into a "Greater Serbia," against the will of the non-Serb majorities there.

These tensions were suppressed during the Cold War, when the rival states were reorganized as constituent republics of communist Yugoslavia. As communist authority weakened in the late 1980s, several of the republics demanded independence. The Serbian leader, Slobodan Milosevic, wished to keep the republics together under Serbian authority, reviving the idea of a Greater Serbia. Serb forces attacked Croatia in 1991 and Bosnia in 1992 in support of the Serb minorities there who rejected independence.

A little girl and her grieving mother sit close together in a Muslim refugee shelter at Zenica. The girl's father was one of the thousands of Muslims executed by Serbs at Srebrenica.

Ethnic cleansing

In Bosnia, Serb forces drove out Bosnian Muslims from the towns and villages they conquered in order to create new areas for Serbs to live. This process was known as "ethnic cleansing." Serb soldiers imprisoned Bosnian Muslim men in concentration camps and raped Bosnian women. The towns the Serbs attacked included some declared "safe havens" by the UN. One of these was Srebrenica.

NATO steps in

The atrocity at Srebrenica sparked international outrage and spurred the world to belated action. In August 1995, NATO war planes began bombing Serbian troops in Bosnia. Milosevic agreed to peace talks, and the Dayton Accord was signed three weeks later. Milosevic was arrested and put on trial for crimes against humanity at an International War Crimes Tribunal in 2001. He died of a heart attack in 2006 before the end of his trial.

Forensic experts from the International War Crimes Tribunal investigate a mass grave. It contains the remains of some of those killed at Srebrenica.

What the papers said

Nobody has behaved honorably in the face of these atrocities. And there were no real lessons learned from Srebrenica. The same thing happened at the beginning of October around Banja Luka. Men were separated from women and children and taken away. Again the West did nothing, despite knowing about it. There are now 2,000 men missing in that area. There's enough guilt to go around. There's blood on everyone's hands here. You're talking about the biggest European war crime in our lifetime.

Time, October 31, 1995

- **SEE ALSO**
  Pages 16–17: April 6, 1994
  Genocide in Rwanda
  Pages 36–37: April 20, 1999
  Massacre at Columbine High School

- **FURTHER INFORMATION**
  - Books:
    The War in Former Yugoslavia by Nathaniel Harris (Wayland, 1997)
  - Websites:
    www.pbs.org/wnet/cryfromthegrave/massacre/massacre.html
    A timeline of events and statements from eyewitnesses

Pokémon Conquer the World

On February 26, 1996, a host of small monsters rushed out of Japan and colonized the whole world, taking over the minds of children. They did not loosen their grip for five years. Pokémon were a series of games and merchandising centering around fictional "pocket monsters." First released in February 1996 as a game for the Nintendo Game Boy, the characters soon appeared in comics, on trading cards, on TV, in books, in two feature films, and on a host of merchandising.

Pokémon became the best-selling computer games and trading cards of all time. The trend encouraged a boom in trading card games, drove sales of handheld games consoles, and brought Japanese anime to a worldwide audience.

Catch 'em all

In the Pokémon game, the player takes on the role of a trainer. He or she aims to collect Pokémon, small monsters of different species that hide in various environments. When a trainer meets a Pokémon, he or she throws a special ball to capture the monster. Captured Pokémon are pitted against others in battles, aiming either to capture them or absorb their strength. Experienced

An employee of Nintendo shows off the newly launched Pokémon game on the Game Boy Color Console.

What the media said

Kids are so eager to collect and trade the products ... that many schools, equally eager to keep their students' attention focused on learning, have declared themselves Pokémon-free zones.... Some parents ... worry that their children are falling into a dangerous world in which fantasy and reality become blurred.

CNN, November 11, 1999

When the Pokémon craze hit New York City, merchandising flooded the stores, along with the electronic games and trading cards.

Pokémon may "evolve" into different, stronger forms. The aim is to collect all the different species and to train a team of powerful Pokémon. In the original game there were 151 Pokémon, but later releases added hundreds more.

Pokémon were invented by the Japanese games engineer Satoshi Tajiri. Inspired by his own love of collecting insects as a child, Tajiri developed the games to give other children the thrill of collecting creatures in a world where cities were largely paved and insects were hard to find.

Game Boys and cards

Pokémon was the first electronic game to appeal to girls and boys equally, and took computer gaming from the realm of geeky boys to a mainstream market. The Nintendo Game Boy, a small, handheld console with its own screen, was released in 1989. As the platform of the Pokémon games, it became the essential toy of the late 1990s. Three million copies of the first Pokémon game were sold in the first three months. But not all children could afford a Game Boy. Trading cards filled the gap, being easily affordable with pocket money. They were so popular that many schools banned them, saying they led to fights and distracted children from lessons. Newspapers even carried stories of children being bullied, robbed, and cheated of their prized cards.

- **SEE ALSO**
  Pages 10–11: August 6, 1991
  The World Wide Web Goes Live

- **FURTHER INFORMATION**
  Websites:
  www.pokemon.com
  The original Pokémon website

Dolly the Sheep Is Born

The birth of a sheep rarely attracts much news coverage. But Dolly was a very special sheep: she was the first mammal cloned from a cell taken from an adult animal. The scientific community was excited about the achievement and what it could mean for the future. Many people, though, worried that cloning was unnatural and that Dolly's birth might pave the way for developments they would find alarming, such as human cloning. Dolly went on to live a pampered life at the Roslin Institute in Scotland, where she was created, but died at the early age of six in 2003.

What the papers said

Now we know that we can clone an adult animal. And since what works in sheep is likely to be possible in humans, we are suddenly propelled right past the imagined techniques of Brave New World…. There are endless possibilities for futuristic speculation. The egotistical may be able to clone themselves and give themselves the upbringing that they always thought they deserved. The rich and powerful would be able to found dynasties where at death they would pass all their wealth to a genetically identical but younger version of themselves.

New Scientist, March 1, 1997

Making copies

A clone is a perfect copy of an animal or plant. Normally, an animal such as a sheep has two parents. Its DNA – the genetic material that acts as the "recipe" for making it – comes from both parents. In a clone, all the DNA comes from one animal. In the case of Dolly, DNA was taken from a cell from the udder of an adult sheep. An egg cell was taken from a different adult sheep. The DNA was removed from the egg cell and all the DNA from the udder cell was put into it instead. The egg was then put into a third sheep to grow normally, being born as a baby sheep on July 5, 1996.

Unnatural interference?

When Dolly's birth was announced in January 1997, it caused some alarm. Many people argue that cloning is wrong or fear that it is dangerous. Some worry that people may be cloned or that babies will be started and used to "harvest" human tissue for medical use. A South Korean group claimed to have created a human baby by cloning in 2002, but it turned out to be a lie. Cloning could be very useful, though. It could help to provide food for a hungry world by producing crops at a much faster rate. Cloning could also produce medicines or even body parts.

Dolly the cloned sheep stands in her stall at the Roslin Institute in Edinburgh. In 1996, Dolly became the first animal to be cloned from DNA taken from an adult animal.

Problems with cloning

Sheep often live 11 or 12 years, and some scientists think that the cloning process may have led to Dolly's early death. Many other cloned mammals have been created since Dolly, and early death and abnormalities are common. It is not clear yet whether these problems will always accompany cloning or whether the techniques currently used are to blame.

- **SEE ALSO**
  Pages 4–5: April 24, 1990
  The Hubble Space Telescope Is Launched
  Pages 20–21: May 6, 1994
  The Channel Tunnel Opens

- **FURTHER INFORMATION**
  Books:
  From Sea Urchins to Dolly the Sheep: Discovering Cloning by Sally Morgan (Heinemann, 2006)
  Websites:
  www.sciencemuseum.org.uk/antenna/dolly/index.asp
  A profile of Dolly the sheep, and the implications of her life and death

Hong Kong Returns to China

Extravagant firework displays, dragon dances, and parties marked the end of more than 100 years of British rule in Hong Kong as the island passed back to Chinese control. The celebrations even included a troupe of dancing children dressed as credit cards – a reference to Hong Kong's status as a thriving financial center. In Beijing, 100,000 invited guests watched on giant television screens set up in Tiananmen Square.

The transfer ceremony took place at the Hong Kong Convention and Exhibition Center moments before midnight on June 30, 1997. Before a crowd of 100,000, Prince Charles, the Prince of Wales, read a farewell speech, then the British and Hong Kong flags were removed and the Chinese flag raised. The last British governor of Hong Kong, Chris Patten, sobbed into his handkerchief. Chinese troops moved into Hong Kong immediately but did nothing to stop the protests that took place in some parts of the island.

Britain's Prince Charles (center), Chris Patten (3rd from right), and Prime Minister Tony Blair (2nd from right) at the Military Farewell Ceremony at the HMS Tamar military base in Hong Kong.

Waiting and worrying

Negotiations for the handover began in 1979. At that time, China was a harsh communist regime – a vast, poor nation strongly opposed to the free market economy that had made Hong Kong rich. The people and businesses of Hong Kong approached the handover with more anxiety than excitement.

Hong Kong is a bustling capitalist marketplace, one of the "tiger economies" of Asia, along with Japan, Singapore, Taiwan, and South Korea. Since 1945, these areas have grown rich making consumer goods

⊙ eye witness

If there is no democracy there will be no rule of law; if there is no freedom, human rights will not be respected.... We want the freedom we are entitled to under the Joint Declaration.

Martin Lee, leader of Hong Kong's Democratic Party

for the West. Many businesses with investments in Hong Kong feared they would suffer following its return to China.

One country, two systems

As the time for the handover approached, the Chinese leader Deng Xiaoping promised that China would be "one country, two systems," with Hong Kong keeping its capitalist status for at least 50 years. This reassured some investors, but many moved out even so. Many Hong Kong residents feared that China would not honor the agreement to allow business in Hong Kong to continue.

To add to Hong Kong's concerns, China had a poor record on human rights, with harsh punishments and an unreliable justice system. After the Tiananmen Square massacre in 1989, when peaceful protestors were mowed down by tanks and guns, the trickle of people leaving Hong Kong turned to a flood. Over a million people left, many going to Britain, the United States, and Canada. But they need not have worried about Hong Kong's economic prospects. During the 1990s and 2000s, China's economy grew from strength to strength. It has opened up to foreign investment and trade, taken on board the capitalist business model, and is now a major economic power.

A spectacular dragon dance formed part of the celebrations at the handover of Hong Kong to China.

- **SEE ALSO**
  Pages 12–13: December 8, 1991
  The End of the Soviet Union
  Pages 18–19: April 27, 1994
  Black Rule in South Africa

- **FURTHER INFORMATION**
- Books:
  Hong Kong by Nicola Barber
  (World Almanac Education, 2004)
- Websites:
  news.bbc.co.uk/onthisday/hi/dates/stories/july/1/newsid_2656000/2656973.stm
  Includes a video of the handover ceremony.

The World Goes Green

On December 11, 1997, the world challenged climate change head on and began an international effort to avoid disaster. On that day, after two and a half years of negotiations, representatives of 150 countries drew up the Kyoto Protocol in Japan. The agreement set targets for reducing emissions of six greenhouse gases by 5 percent of 1990 levels by 2012.

The protocol built on the work of the Framework Convention on Climate Change of 1992. The convention encouraged countries to reduce their carbon emissions, whereas the protocol set out to force reductions. Developed countries were to reduce their greenhouse gas emissions immediately. Developing countries must monitor and report emissions, but need not cut them. Each developed country has its own target for reducing emissions, tailored to its needs and capabilities. For example, the European Union overall must reduce emissions by 8 percent; Canada must cut emissions by 6 percent.

Instead of reducing emissions, a country can find a partner for "carbon trading." By buying greenhouse gas allowance from a country that does not use all its allowance, a more extravagant country can continue to produce carbon emissions above its target.

What the papers said

Negotiators from more than 150 countries flew out of Kyoto, Japan, this week after agreeing only the weakest of compromises to combat global warming. A host of unresolved issues remain, each of which could yet make the agreement unworkable.... Some issues were left out of the deal altogether. These included emissions from aircraft and shipping, which make up as much as 5 percent of global CO_2 [carbon dioxide – a greenhouse gas] emissions but remain outside any control agreement.

New Scientist, December 13, 1997

Climate change and carbon emissions

Global temperatures are rising, and this has begun to affect the natural world. Most scientists agree that the rise in greenhouse gases in the atmosphere is causing the temperature to rise, with potentially disastrous consequences for the world's population. Greenhouse gases are produced by burning fossil fuels such as coal, oil, and gas and by intensive farming. Greenhouse gases trap the sun's heat within the atmosphere, thus raising global temperatures.

Young Japanese people protest against global warming in front of delegates to the UN conference on climate change in Kyoto.

In 1997, not everyone agreed that climate change was the result of human activities. Some countries used this doubt as a reason not to accept the agreement. The United States refused to sign the Kyoto Protocol, as did Australia. Politicians in these countries feared that cutting carbon emissions would damage trade and industry. They also wanted large developing countries to limit their own emissions. The United States withdrew completely from the discussions in 2001 after George W. Bush became president.

After Kyoto

Kyoto was only the start. The agreement would not come into force until enough high-emitting countries had signed it. This target had been met by late 2004, and the Kyoto agreement came into force on February 15, 2005. Several countries are on target for meeting the reductions they need to make by 2012.

- **FURTHER INFORMATION**
- 📖 **Books:**
  An Inconvenient Truth: Young Adult Version by Al Gore (Bloomsbury, 2007)

  What If We Do Nothing? Global Warming by Neil Morris (Watts, 2007)
- **Websites:**
  www.climatechallenge.gov.uk
  A British government website that offers a simple, clear guide to climate change.

Massacre at Columbine High School

Students cowered under tables as two of their colleagues, Eric Harris and Dylan Klebold, sprayed them with bullets from automatic rifles. For nearly an hour the two killers rampaged through Columbine High School in Denver, Colorado, killing 13 people and injuring 24. Terrified students and staff tried to hide as the attackers began shooting outside, then moved into the cafeteria and finished with a massacre of students taking shelter under tables in the library. The gunmen shot themselves before police arrived. In addition to a range of guns, the killers used bombs of various types, many of which failed to detonate properly. At the time, it was the third deadliest school massacre in U.S. history.

Pupils at Columbine High School comfort each other following the massacre.

Games and guns

The immediate public response in the United States was outrage. How could the boys have gathered so many weapons, made bombs, collected ammunition, and planned their assault without anyone noticing? And what led them to kill their fellow students? Some people blamed the gun culture in the United States, saying that the ready availability of guns made it too easy for the killers to collect weapons. Others blamed violent computer games and videos for desensitizing the boys. Both students had been avid players of violent computer games. Harris had been banned from using the computer at home as a punishment for bad behavior. Some people thought he turned to violence when he could not express his anger and frustration in a game.

Harris and Klebold had previously been arrested for stealing weapons. Harris posted entries on his blog listing the guns he had and the people he wanted to kill. He then made threats of violence toward students and staff at the school. Although the police knew about the website, they took no action.

Other school massacres

School massacres are rare outside the United States. Britain's only school massacre was in Dunblane, Scotland. On March 13, 1996, Thomas Hamilton killed 15 children and a teacher in Dunblane primary school. Hamilton was not killing fellow students, though. He was an adult with no direct connection with the school he targeted. In 1993, a gunman took six children and an adult hostage in a nursery school in Paris, France, and demanded a ransom of $18.5 million.

This is a still from a home video made some six weeks before the massacre. It shows Eric Harris (left) and Dylan Klebold at a makeshift shooting range in Douglas County, Colorado.

What the papers said

So the violence is over. Innocents are dead. The perpetrators are dead. The survivors are scarred. The rest of us wonder why. Is the ever-ready limelight of news coverage creating a self-replicating youth trend – massacre chic?... But one eyewitness account seems to drive home the futility of reasoned solutions. "They were laughing after they shot," said Columbine student Aaron Cohn. "It was like they were having the time of their life." And they were. No solution to *that*, except to wait for the next time, and hope it never comes.

Time, April 21, 1999

- **SEE ALSO**
  Pages 22–23: March 20, 1995
  Nerve Gas Attack on the Tokyo Subway
  Pages 26–27: July 12, 1995
  Massacre at Srebrenica
  Pages 40–41: April 19, 1995
  The Oklahoma City Bombing

- **FURTHER INFORMATION**
  📖 Books:
  Columbine High School Shooting: Student Violence by Judy L. Hasday (Enslow, 2002)
  🎬 Movies:
  Bowling for Columbine written and directed by Michael Moore (2002)

31 DECEMBER 1999

Millennium Fever

Around the world, firework displays, free concerts, and massive public parties marked the end of the millennium at midnight on December 31, 1999. Celebrations took place in a wave as midnight arrived at different places around the world, beginning with the uninhabited Millennium Island in the middle of the Pacific. Sunrise on Millennium Island on January 1, 2000 was televised around the world.

Party like it's 1999

Many countries built lasting structures, such as bridges, pavilions, sports stadiums and parks to mark the new millennium. There were also many temporary structures and exhibitions, such as the Millennium Exhibition in the Millennium Dome in London, England, and La Grande Roue, a large ferris wheel in La Place de la Concorde in Paris, France.

Although the new millennium was celebrated on January 1, 2000, many people argued that it would actually start in 2001. As the calendar has no "year 0," the first millennium was 1–1000, the second millennium 1001–2000.

The millennium bug

While most people celebrated, some worried that computer programs would go wrong, perhaps with catastrophic results, or that terrorists would try to attack. A few religious groups even believed the world would come to an end.

Many computer programs written during the 1980s and earlier had no way of storing a year for the date that contained more than two digits. So the year 1995, for instance, would be shown as "95." At the start of the year 2000, the year would be stored as "00" and the computer would assume it meant 1900. Experts warned that if the problem was not fixed, planes might fall out of

What the papers said

Two thousand years after Christ's obscure birth in a dusty town in Judea, the world's 6 billion people ... rode their turning blue planet across time's invisible line today and, by common consent, looked into the dawn of a new millennium.... What they saw first was a party. It was garish, glittering and global, and millions, setting religious considerations and personal concerns aside, joined in the festivities to celebrate the conjunction of a new year, a new century and a new thousand-year cycle of history. They also put aside the inconvenient fact that the millennium, technically, is still a year off.

New York Times, January 1, 2000

Christians celebrate the millennium in front of the Church of the Nativity in Bethlehem, the city traditionally regarded as the birthplace of Jesus.

the sky (since their systems would register that they had not yet taken off), power stations would fail, and untold numbers of computer-controlled processes would stop or go wrong. The potential for disaster seemed huge.

Around the world, organizations and governments invested billions of dollars in converting all their computer programs to recognize four-digit dates, so that "2000" clearly came after "1999." As the hour of midnight approached on December 31, 1999, the world held its breath. In fact, there were very few problems. This may have been because of the actions taken, or the problem might have been overstated – it will never be clear.

• **FURTHER INFORMATION**

📖 Books:
The Story of Clocks and Calendars: Marking a Millennium by Betsy Maestro (William Morrow, 2000)

🖱 Websites:
news.bbc.co.uk/1/hi/world/asia-pacific/583585.stm
A report on festivities and fears that accompanied the dawn of the new millennium.

19
APRIL
1995

The Oklahoma City Bombing

On the morning of April 19, 1995, it was business as usual at the Alfred P. Murrah Federal Building in Oklahoma City, Oklahoma. Most of the people employed at the building – which housed offices of various government agencies – had reported for work. Most of the children had been dropped off at the day care center on the second floor. Suddenly, at 9:02 A.M., a huge explosion ripped through the building. At the time, it was the worst terrorist attack ever to occur on U.S. soil.

The Alfred P. Murrah Federal Building in Oklahoma City one day after the bombing.

A Devastating Explosion

The explosion left a 20-foot (6.1-meter) wide, 8-foot (2.4-m) deep crater in the street and damaged or destroyed more than 300 nearby structures, as well as destroying much of the nine-story Murrah Federal Building. Frantic efforts immediately began to rescue those trapped inside. In the end, 168 people died, including 19 children, and hundreds were injured. The explosion was caused by a bomb left in a truck parked in front of the building. Many people assumed that international terrorists were responsible for the explosion. However, the bomb had been set by a domestic terrorist – a former U.S. Army soldier named Timothy McVeigh. Ninety minutes after the explosion, a state trooper stopped McVeigh while he was driving north of Oklahoma City because his car did not have a license plate. He was arrested for having a concealed weapon.

On April 20, investigators at the scene of the explosion found the rear axle and remains of a license plate from a Ryder truck. They traced the truck to a Kansas rental agency, where workers helped federal agents create a sketch of the man who had rented the truck. Hotel employees identified the picture as that of McVeigh – who was still under arrest. Investigators soon learned much about him. McVeigh wanted revenge for the way the U.S. government had handled confrontations with anti-government groups that had ended in violence and bloodshed. With the help of a friend, Terry Nichols, he had collected the supplies needed to build a bomb and decided where to plant it. On the morning of April 19, he drove to the Murrah Federal Building, parked the truck, and lit the timed fuses on the bomb. Then he drove away in the getaway car he had left nearby.

Trials and Aftermath

McVeigh was put on trial in Denver, Colorado. On June 2, 1997, a jury found him guilty of murder and conspiracy. He was sentenced to death and was executed on June 11, 2001. Terry Nichols was arrested and also put on trial. He was found guilty and sentenced to life in prison. The remains of the Murrah Federal Building were demolished on May 23, 1995. Five years later, the Oklahoma City National Memorial was dedicated on the site.

Unfortunately, terrorist acts did not end. After the events of September 11, 2001 – when terrorists hijacked four planes and crashed them into the World Trade Center, the Pentagon, and a field in Pennsylvania – the Oklahoma City bombing fell to second place in the list of worst terrorist attacks in the United States.

Timothy McVeigh, pictured after his sentencing. He never expressed any remorse for the bombing.

What the papers said

Oklahoma City will never be the same. This is a place, after all, where terrorists don't venture. . . . Car bombs don't kill children here. Wednesday changed everything. In an explosion felt at least 15 miles away, the fresh, innocent morning turned to horror.

The Oklahoman, April 20, 1995

- **SEE ALSO**
  Pages 22–23: March 20, 1995
  Nerve Gas Attack on the Tokyo Subway

- **FURTHER INFORMATION**
  📖 Books:
  The Oklahoma City Bombing by Richard Brownell (Lucent Books, 2007)
  🖱 Websites:
  www.oklahomacitynationalmemorial.org
  The Oklahoma City National Memorial & Museum

The Million Man March

In the mid-1990s, many believed that the African American community was in trouble. The crime rate and the incidence of drug addiction were high among African American men. Many young blacks were dropping out of school. Poverty and unemployment were common. One out of every three black men in their twenties was in jail, on parole, or on probation. Minister Louis Farrakhan, the leader of a religious group called the Nation of Islam, decided that the time was right to call on African American men to work to change things.

The Call Goes Out

Farrakhan called for "a day of atonement" during which black men would commit themselves to rejecting destructive behaviors. They would dedicate themselves to work toward unity, improved education, and spiritual and moral renewal. October 16, 1995 was the date set for the Million Man March, a huge rally that would take place on the National Mall in Washington, D.C. Farrakhan was a controversial figure who had been accused of being anti-Semitic and anti-white, and many people refused to participate in a gathering associated with him. Some women were also upset because they were excluded. Despite this, many African American leaders took part in the march, including Reverend Jesse Jackson.

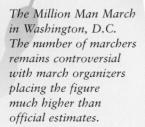

The Million Man March in Washington, D.C. The number of marchers remains controversial with march organizers placing the figure much higher than official estimates.

eye witness

What happens back home will determine whether this massive event had a lasting effect, or was just an emotional celebration that lasted no more than one day.
Bob Franken, reporting for CNN, October 16, 1995

A participant at the Million Man March on the National Mall. The Mall had been the site of many famous demonstrations in U.S. history, including the 1963 March on Washington for civil rights, led by Martin Luther King, Jr.

Hundreds of thousands of African American men assembled in Washington, many arriving by bus. Activities began with prayers at 6 A.M. The day was full of speeches by religious and educational leaders and talks on the importance of self-respect and taking responsibility. The mood was upbeat, with cheers and applause, bands playing, and African song and dance. A speech by Farrakhan, lasting more than two hours, concluded the program. According to one estimate, more than 800,000 people attended the march.

Significance of the March

The Million Man March was one of the largest demonstrations to take place in Washington. In the years after the march, significant problems remained in the African American community, but there were some positive effects. More than 1 million black men registered to vote in the months following the march, and membership increased in African American religious, social service, and political organizations. A program encouraging African American families to adopt black children showed great success.

Another march was held in Washington on October 15, 2005 by the Millions More Movement, a coalition of African American leaders, to mark the tenth anniversary of the Million Man March. This time, the march was open to men, women, and children. The focus was on creating lasting relationships among individuals, religious organizations, and community groups.

- **FURTHER INFORMATION**
- 📖 Books:
  One Million Strong: A Photographic Tribute to the Million Man March and Affirmations for the African American Male by Roderick Terry (Duncan & Duncan, 1996)
- 🖱 Websites:
  www.cnn.com/US/9510/megamarch/march.html CNN's website on the Million Man March, with stories about the march, film clips, and background information

The President Is Impeached

Bill Clinton, a Democrat, became president of the United States in January 1993. Despite Clinton's success in improving the economy and other matters, his presidency was clouded by accusations of both personal and financial wrongdoing. As a result of those charges, on December 19, 1998, Clinton was impeached by the U.S. House of Representatives.

A Lengthy Investigation

During the fall of 1993, the president and his wife, Hillary Rodham Clinton, were accused of possible misconduct in their dealings in the Whitewater Development Corporation, an Arkansas land-development firm. In 1994, Kenneth Starr was appointed as independent counsel to look into the matter. Starr was a fervent Republican, and many Democrats and Clinton supporters claimed the Republicans were unfairly targeting the Clintons. Starr began a four-year investigation of the president, during which he learned that, beginning in late 1995, Clinton had engaged in a sexual relationship with a young woman named Monica Lewinsky who worked at the White House. In January 1998, Starr got permission to expand the Whitewater investigation to determine if Clinton had lied under oath about the affair and tried to influence the testimony of others about it. At first, Clinton denied the affair, but in August 1998, he admitted it on national television.

President Clinton at a press conference on January 26, 1998, when he denied having sexual relations with Monica Lewinsky.

The Impeachment Proceedings

In September, Starr delivered his report to the House of Representatives. The Judiciary Committee authorized an inquiry into impeaching the president, which could result in his being removed from office. According to the U.S. Constitution, the House is responsible for starting impeachment proceedings, while the Senate is responsible for conducting the actual trial. On December 19, the House approved two articles of impeachment, accusing the president of having committed perjury (lying) before a grand jury and obstruction of justice. It was only the second time in U.S. history that a president was impeached. Andrew Johnson was impeached in 1868 and found not guilty by one vote.

Clinton's trial began in the Senate on January 7, 1999. The president's defenders argued that lying about sexual matters was a private concern and was not an abuse of governmental authority, while his accusers said that he had broken the law and undermined the integrity of his office. The trial lasted until February 12, when the Senate voted. On the first article, perjury, 45 senators voted for impeachment and 55 against. On the second article, obstruction of justice, the vote was tied, 50–50. Both votes – which fell far short of the two-thirds needed for conviction – were conducted along party lines, with no Democrats voting to convict the president.

The impeachment trial in the United States Senate, presided over by Chief Justice William Rehnquist (center rear). Following his acquittal, Clinton said he was "profoundly sorry" and called for a "time of reconciliation and renewal for America."

Throughout the investigation and proceedings, most Americans were against impeachment and gave Clinton high job approval ratings while also criticizing his personal conduct. Clinton remained influential and politically active after he left office. He encouraged his wife to run for the Senate in 2000 and helped her campaign (unsuccessfully) for the 2008 Democratic nomination as president. His prominence is likely to continue following Hillary Clinton's appointment as U.S. secretary of state in the administration of President Barack Obama.

● eye witness

Many Americans voiced anger, disgust and frustration with the proceedings. Some radiated grim satisfaction. But as President Clinton's long, painful journey from scandal to impeachment ended yesterday, most Americans were just benumbed, inoculated by the seemingly endless months of lies, legalisms and disillusionment with politics.

New York Times, December 20, 1998

• FURTHER INFORMATION

📖 **Books:**

An Affair of State: The Investigation, Impeachment, and Trial of President Clinton by Richard A. Posner (Harvard University Press, 1999)

Bill Clinton by Michael Benson (Lerner Publications, 2003)

The Impeachment of William Jefferson Clinton by Daniel Cohen (Twenty-first Century Books, 2000)

🖱 **Websites:**

www.pbs.org/newshour/impeachment/index.html The Impeachment Trial, a PBS Online NewsHour website devoted to President Clinton's impeachment, with analysis and statements from participants

People of the Decade

Aung San Suu Kyi
(1945–)
Aung San Suu Kyi is leader of the National League for Democracy in Burma. She leads a peaceful, non-violent struggle against the military dictatorship in Burma. She has been under house arrest in Burma, on the orders of the country's military rulers, since 1989. She has been freed and rearrested several times. Suu Kyi is considered by the National League for Democracy to be the legitimate prime minister of Burma. She won the Nobel Prize for Peace in 1991.

Bill Clinton
(1946–)
Bill Clinton was the 42nd president of the United States, in office 1993–2001. Although his presidency was marred by scandals and indictment for perjury (of which he was cleared), he retained international popularity. He presided over the longest period of peacetime economic growth in the United States since 1945 and made substantial efforts to broker peace in the Middle East. His policies at home included improving the education system and providing healthcare and job prospects. Internationally, he authorized the use of U.S. troops as part of a NATO force in Yugoslavia.

Kurt Cobain
(1967–1994)
American guitarist, singer, and songwriter Kurt Cobain co-founded the iconic alternative band Nirvana in 1987. Nirvana was hugely successful, bringing to the fore the music of the Seattle "grunge" scene. Cobain suffered from bronchitis and stomach pains all his life and became addicted to heroin, which he claimed eased his physical pain. He killed himself in 1994. By this time, Nirvana had become one of the most popular and influential bands of the era.

Bill Gates
(1955–)
Bill Gates is an American businessman and computer pioneer and one of the richest people in the world. He established the computer company Microsoft in 1975. Gates produced the operating system DOS used by IBM PCs, and in 1985, Microsoft launched the first version of Windows. Microsoft went on to dominate the software industry with its main products, Windows and Microsoft Office, used worldwide. Gates has given billions of dollars for charitable causes through the foundations he has set up.

Saddam Hussein
(1937–2006)
Saddam Hussein was president of Iraq from 1979–2003. He created a repressive security force that gave him a powerful hold on the country. During the 1990s, his invasion of Kuwait, attacks on his own people, and refusal to cooperate with UN weapons inspectors made him an enemy of the West and especially of the United States. He was deposed in 2003 following an invasion of Iraq by a U.S.-led coalition. He was convicted of illegally killing Shi'ite opponents and executed in 2006.

Helmut Kohl
(1930–)
Helmut Kohl was chancellor of Germany from 1982 to 1998. As one of the most influential European politicians of the second half of the 20th century, he oversaw the reunification of Germany in 1990. Kohl worked with President François Mitterand of France to push through the Maastricht Treaty (1992), which created the European Union. He was also instrumental in the introduction of the Euro, the European currency now used in 15 member states.

Nelson Mandela
(1918–)
Nelson Mandela became the first black president of South Africa following the country's first fully democratic elections in 1994. He was active in the anti-apartheid movement of the African National Congress (ANC) from 1952. In 1962, he was arrested and imprisoned for 27 years. He gained international support as the figurehead of the the the anti-apartheid cause, which he continued to champion from prison. He was released from prison in 1990 and won the Nobel Prize for Peace in 1993.

J. K. Rowling
(1965–)
British writer Joanne Rowling is the author of the "Harry Potter" novels, which took the publishing world by storm in the 1990s. Rowling became the best-selling children's novelist of all time, with all seven of the books in the series topping the bestseller lists and titles four to seven breaking sales records on their release. The Potter novels built a substantial following, further increased by the release of the films of the books beginning in 2001. Rowling is ranked the 12th richest woman in Britain.

Boris Yeltsin
(1931–2007)
The first president of the Russian Federation, 1991–1999, Yeltsin promised reforms that would bring economic renewal to Russia. However, his attempts at turning the ex-communist state into a free market economy failed dismally. Privatization and free pricing enabled a handful of businesspeople to enrich themselves while leaving vast numbers in poverty. Corruption and violent crime were rife in Yeltsin's Russia, and on several occasions the country teetered on the brink of economic collapse.

Glossary

anti-Semite A person who dislikes and discriminates against Jews.

capitalist A system in which trade and industry are controlled by private owners for profit.

coalition Two or more political parties that have agreed to work together.

communist A system, or the belief in a system, in which capitalism is overthrown and the state controls wealth and property.

confederation A group of states acting together.

democracy A system of government in which the leaders have been elected freely and equally by all the citizens of a country, or a country with such a system.

detonate Set off an explosive device.

dormant Inactive.

economic sanctions Financial methods of making a rogue state comply with the wishes of other states, including refusing to trade or imposing high taxes on the state's exports.

emissions Gases released as a product of natural or human activity.

eruption (volcanic) The rapid outpouring of hot gases, ash, and lava from a volcano.

forensic Relating to the investigation of crime by examining physical evidence in detail, often using scientific methods.

free market economy An economic system in which the price of goods and services is allowed to find its own level as dictated by supply and demand.

genocide The killing of, or the attempt to kill, a whole race of people.

greenhouse gases Carbon gases that help to trap heat near the earth, causing the planet to warm up.

Holocaust The Nazis' genocidal campaign (1942–1945) to exterminate all Jews.

humanitarian Describing something done benevolently, in the interests of humankind.

impeachment The process of bringing formal charges against someone, such as a president or a judge, for having committed serious crimes or being guilty of significant misconduct.

independent counsel In the United States, an individual appointed by a panel of judges to investigate accusations of serious wrongdoing by a federal official.

indictment A formal charge of having committed a crime.

mafia A large, organized criminal gang.

mandate An official authorization to rule.

merchandising Consumer goods licensed with a brand or character.

nationalist Supportive of the right of one's people to exist as a nation, or belief in the status of one's nation above all others.

Ottoman Empire An empire under the control of Turkey until the end of World War I.

paramilitary Describing an organization that uses a military structure, weapons, and tactics and fights within a country, usually against the government.

parole The early release of a prisoner, who for a set period of time is supposed to maintain good behavior and regularly report to the authorities.

perjury The crime of lying under oath in court.

probation A period of supervision of a criminal offender who instead of going to prison may go free but must regularly report to a probation officer.

protocol A formal agreement between nations.

puppet regime A government installed by and under the control of an external power.

rabies A viral infection of animals that can be passed on to humans and is usually fatal.

reconciliation The ending of a conflict or renewal of friendly relations between people, groups, or countries.

red giant A star in the late stages of its life when it grows very large and glows red.

referendum A vote by the whole of an electorate on a particular question put to it by a government.

refugee A person who has fled from his or her home because of a natural disaster, war, or other catastrophe.

republic A state with a form of government in which supreme power is in the hands of representatives elected by the people.

sarin An extremely poisonous gas that attacks the central nervous system, causing convulsions and death.

sect A small, close-knit group with strongly held views, sometimes viewed as extreme by most people.

sediment Solid matter deposited by or in a liquid.

shanty town A settlement of rough, often temporary, buildings or huts inhabited by very poor people.

Soviet Union Also known as the USSR, a country consisting of Russia and a number of other East European, Baltic, and Central Asian countries. The Soviet Union existed from 1922 to 1991.

tiger economy Any of several states in Southeast Asia that underwent rapid economic growth during the second half of the 20th century.

township In apartheid South Africa, townships were urban settlements planned for black people only, usually with inferior facilities and services.

toxin Poison.

tsar A ruler of the Russian Empire.

Index

Page numbers in **bold** refer to illustrations